T0110913

LOSING SIGHT BUT NOT VISION

Go All the Way

Dr. John D. McConnell

authorHOUSE·

AuthorHouse™
1663 Liberty Drive
Bloomington, IN 47403
www.authorhouse.com
Phone: 833-262-8899

Published by AuthorHouse 07/25/2023

ISBN: 979-8-8230-1004-7 (sc)
ISBN: 979-8-8230-1003-0 (e)

Library of Congress Control Number: 2023910977

Print information available on the last page.

This book is printed on acid-free paper.

DEDICATION

This book is dedicated to those who have transformed pain into testimony, lack into surplus, and desolation into triumph. When I slip into bouts of despair, I am thankful that I am not without examples to aspire to. Your names are many, and your contributions are boundless. I dedicate the many hours invested in this book to those challenged with emotional, mental, and physical disabilities. You fight every day, not only to live, but for the chance to live again. Thank you to those who have held the spotlight (Stevie Wonder, Michael J Fox, John Nash, Stephen Hawking, Dr. Maya Angelo, Ray Charles, Frida Kahlo) making living with disabilities look easy. It's nothing we ask for, but also nothing we shy away from. This book is also dedicated to those who champion legislation like the Americans with Disabilities Act, to protect the civil liberties of those with disabilities.

INTRODUCTION

When I was a schoolteacher, I used an icebreaker called 'four corners' to begin each semester. The facilitator outlines four descriptors for participants to choose from. The objective is to stand under the banner that best resembles you. Essentially, it's a way of grouping people using labels. Labels are fun in game situations, but in life – not so much. Attached to labels are expectations shrouded with prejudice. Somehow, moving beyond them has become the burden of the labeled, rather than the other way around. Even if you've never consented to that particular designation, it's on you to alter the perception. Rather than wasting an exorbitant amount of time trying to change a narrative, invest your energy to reach your goals. We have a limited amount of time on this earth, and perhaps an even smaller sphere of influence. Once we can accept that life has many curveballs to throw, we can take the position that nothing will stop us from completing our mission. A label is only as accurate as how well it defines your actions.

A disciplined visionary can go further having a disability, than anyone unwilling to set goals. It's important to understand the difference between having a disability and being a disabled person. Only you determine if you are a disabled person. If you are currently standing under that banner, please allow this book to germinate new thoughts and generate a fresh new rigor to your daily life. Your mental, and or physical dexterity may be compromised, but if you are willing to consider the possibilities, your dreams can still thrive. How much do you have the capacity to see? Robert H. Schuller said, "Any fool can count the number of seeds in an apple. Only God can count all the apples in one seed". Allow this manuscript to assist you in moving beyond self-imposed limitations, and towards unsuspecting optimism. Transform your suffering into your strength.

FOREWORD
by
Dr. Mark A. McConnell

In a world brimming with distractions, challenges, and setbacks, it is easy to lose sight of our true potential. We find ourselves entangled in the web of limitations, allowing circumstances, disabilities, or self-doubt to dictate the boundaries of our lives. But there are remarkable individuals who refuse to succumb to such limitations, who transcend the physical or psychological barriers that threaten to shatter their dreams. This book is a tribute to their unwavering spirit and their relentless pursuit of disciplined vision.

"Losing Sight But Not Vision" is a profound exploration of the extraordinary power that lies within each of us—the power to set goals, rise above adversity, and transform our lives. It is a testament to the strength of the human spirit, illuminating the path for anyone facing adversity, regardless of their background or circumstances.

Within these pages, you will encounter stories of triumph over adversity, resilience in the face of daunting challenges, and the unwavering determination of individuals who refused to let anything hold them back. Through their experiences, you will discover the profound truth that vision is not merely an act of seeing, but a deeply rooted force that fuels the human spirit. It is an indomitable flame that persists even when the world around us grows dark.

This book invites you to embark on a transformative journey, one that transcends the boundaries of physical sight and delves into the core of human potential. You will witness the awe-inspiring achievements of those who have overcome disabilities, societal constraints, and personal doubts, proving that our vision is not confined to the mere use of our eyes, but rather, it resides within the depths of our souls.

"Losing Sight But Not Vision" challenges conventional notions of success and inspires us to redefine the limitations we place upon ourselves. It reminds us that the human spirit is boundless, capable of achieving greatness even in the face of seemingly insurmountable obstacles. Through the stories shared within these pages, you will gain the tools to unleash your own disciplined vision, cultivating an unwavering resolve that propels you forward towards your dreams.

Let this book be your guide, an illumination in moments of darkness, a source of inspiration when faced with adversity. May it empower you to redefine what is possible, emboldening you to forge a path unburdened by fear or doubt. With every turn of the page, may you discover that the true essence of vision lies not in our physical sight but in the limitless capacity of our hearts and minds.

Together, let us embark on this extraordinary journey and embrace the profound truth that no disability, no setback, and no challenge can extinguish the flame of our dreams. Let us celebrate the triumph of the human spirit, as we strive to lose sight of the limitations that bind us and ignite the unyielding fire of our disciplined vision.

With unwavering hope and boundless possibilities,

Dr. Mark A. McConnell

CONTENTS

CHAPTER 1

SETTING YOUR SIGHTS

Believe it or not, life's playing field is level for all. Only certain demographics of people are allowed to say this in public without retribution. If you are adorned in a certain skin color, and perceived as having no handicaps, you'd be ridiculed for making such a statement. Even when we think we know one another, the best we can do is catch a person's vibe. We spend our entire lives on a mission to find ourselves - yet there are people who say they know us well.

I'll preface this story by saying I shouldn't have been driving. One morning I pulled up to the gym and parked in the handicap spot closest to the entrance. Another gym patron who looked to be at least fifteen years my senior was arriving at the same time, and opened the door for me. As we entered, we shared pleasantries and then he said, "You don't look handicapped". He obviously noticed where I'd parked, and watched me walk to the entrance without a hitch in my step. I didn't owe him a response, but I gestured to my eyes. Very sarcastically he responded, "Yeah…, right…" I spent nearly two hours on the treadmill, and about every twenty minutes this same man walked directly in front of me, shaking his head in a condescending manner. I'm sure he felt that on some level he was advocating for people with disabilities. He was attempting to make me feel guilty for using a handicap placard he obviously didn't believe I deserved. But what wasn't obvious to him was the fact that

I am legally blind. He, like many others, based his opinion on what was seemingly apparent. From the moment he saw me park my vehicle, he was expecting an identifier to reveal itself that I'm unwell (not whole, broken). What do you consider to be a deficit in terms of an impairment? When did it become a requirement to announce our struggles? Must those who are weak provide disclaimers to make those who are strong feel comfortable? Guess what – we all struggle with something! Yes, we can grow to an acceptance of the baggage that comes along with our challenges. However, the best chance you have of being treated "normal" is by blending in and not shining an unwanted spotlight on yourself.

Allow me to qualify my opening statement, "Life's playing field is level for all". The human condition is just that - conditions comprised of strengths and weaknesses we must learn to navigate. Just as in a vehicle, navigation is hindered without first being able to appreciate where you are. What do you have? What are your strengths? Unless confronted by the right situation, the majority of the 8 billion people on earth don't know the extent of their power. Our adrenal glands attempt to keep pace with our body's stress by releasing chemicals into the bloodstream for optimal adaptation. ABC streams a recurring human-interest show called "What Would You Do?" Actors fictitiously create a confrontational scenario in a public venue, in view of unsuspecting bystanders. John Quiñones, the host, comes out at the end of the exchange - making it apparent that it's just a gag. He then interviews the bystanders to find out why they responded the way they did. It's unrealistic to think we'll make it through life without confrontation, struggles, discomfort, and trials - but I believe the average person tries to avoid those situations as much as possible.

When I mention "blending in", I'm not referring to dumbing down who you are. Keep in mind that when people don't know you, that's exactly how they interact with you – as a stranger. Some encounters we have with people will be momentary; pumping gas at a gas station, standing in line in a grocery store. Depending on our battle, the half can't be told in a one-minute exchange. So, focus on the best outcome possible from an elevator speech. Not forcing your entire story isn't being fake, it's considerate. People can't truly appreciate your story without the knowledge of who you are anyway.

Where you end up is determined by the goals you set for yourself. I try to set my sights above where I actually think I can land. Norman Vincent Peale said, "Shoot for the moon. Even if you miss you may land amongst the stars".

As the world's population increases, so do the forms of discrimination. Though we've experienced stellar attributes in our evolution as human beings, our threshold for judging one another remains rather archaic and barbaric. Avoiding and ignoring who and what we don't understand seems more important than loving people. No matter the race, gender, sexual preference, physical or mental impairment, age, origin of birth, socioeconomic status, religion, etc..., people are people first. If everyone found "acceptance" at the level of their desire, this would be a different kind of world. Let's be clear. Tolerance and acceptance is not what this book is about. These words are to move you from where you are, to where you want to be - despite your being tolerated or accepted. In most cases, acceptance usually follows understanding. You can literally lose years of life trying to get people to understand. My message is to LIVE WITHOUT PERMISSION!

Although we may have some of the very same experiences, our take-away will be different. Every experience makes an imprint; however, the host determines how extensively the grooves are carved. We don't get to determine the significance of each moment, but the perspectives we take from them are totally our responsibility. Relating to the opportunity of a life altering experience is an important role every individual should embrace. There is so much more to our daily encounters than what we see at first glance. Commit to extract the full measure from every interaction. Even the thoughts that come during alone-time are worth jotting down. If you look hard enough, you can trace the lines and find priceless connections. If we are not impacting a situation, perhaps the situation is designed to impact us. Don't walk away unaffected. Lend yourself to the process.

I don't want a life that's full of regret. Knowing I've done my due diligence is very important to me. From how I vacation, to the types of food I enjoy, I want to experiment, investigate, and know just as much about what I don't like as what I'm drawn to. When it comes to things we are ignorant about, it's important to give ourselves the best vantage point. Offering intelligent opinions is difficult, if you're clueless regarding the subject matter.

Casting vision for one's self, must be implemented in stages, or else it's too large to manage. The assignments I give myself for prolonging physical health have to be separated from my other ambitions. Improving my networking skills as a 'businessman' is futile, unless the businessman remains healthy enough to thrive in the physical world. There is a sensible chain reaction that promotes growth when in the right sequence.

The reduction of an ability does not necessarily translate into the absence of the ability. Certain life events can be very traumatic. An unexpected diagnosis at the doctor's office, or personally discovering a growth, lump, or abnormality in the mirror can set us on a pathway of fear. The mind drafts a script of the worst-case scenario - the one that doesn't portray you with vitality. Be careful not to embrace a negative perspective for your life, even if someone tries to assign one to you.

We create our truth every day. We frame our world with our own expectations. Always give yourself something to aim for, rather than something to pull back from. It may be true that there are new barriers to overcome, but don't allow the threat of the barrier to be your limitation.

Let's take a moment to practice bashing negative reports without denying their legitimacy. The blood test may support the symptoms you feel, but that's no reason to be hopeless. Your energy may be compromised due to your challenge, but forward thinking can assist you in modifying your workload. Perhaps your body will no longer allow you to excel doing things the way you're accustomed - so take this time to re-tool with new strategies. It's true that tasks may have become more difficult, but with the creativity and wisdom from God, you can do all things through Christ, who strengthens you.

Always be ready to counter something negative with something positive. It's not doubt or a lack of faith to have responses prepared. It's a good strategy to empower us to be responders and not reactors. Reacting is something we do because something occurred. Responding is something we do regardless of something occurring. We've lived long enough to realize that we will always have things to overcome. Part of how I overcome, are the confessions I consistently declare. Even before something negative rears its head, I'm already saturating my atmosphere with scriptures. "The wealth of the sinner is laid up for the just" (Proverbs 13:22). "The joy of the Lord is my strength" (Nehemiah 8:10). "No weapon formed against you shall prosper, And every tongue *which* rises against you in judgment You shall condemn" (Isaiah 54:17). "Riches and honor are mine to give. So are wealth and lasting success" (Proverbs 8:18). "I do what is right and follow the path of justice" (Proverbs 8:20). The best offense is to deploy an even better defense. Strive to become powerful with your words. You're not instigating trouble to come by preparing for it. You are using wisdom by saying to trouble, "I know you're coming". If you stay ready, there's no need to get ready.

CHAPTER 2

CONTINUING DESPITE THE ODDS

How do you go beyond the feeling of despair? After repeatedly entering contests and never placing, auditioning with no callback, and applying for positions never awarded to you - when is it enough? It's so hard to know if I'm chasing an unfathomable dream when it seems people with less talent get the nod. There used to be rules, and you had to pay your dues. Rules no longer apply. The variables range from "who you know", to "the right timing", and everything in between. So how does one remain enthused about the journey when the road is paved with detours?

I've always believed that it's easy to take things for granted when they come without much effort. Everyone desires a 'turn-key' situation, that's free of struggle and fight. But truthfully, we have more appreciation for things we've worked to obtain. If you are fortunate enough to know what you're truly passionate about, resistance shouldn't dim your path. Our strategies and methods must shift to reflect the industry we are targeting, but the fire in your belly should be a constant if it's truly the vision for your life. A better question might be, "Am I chasing the right thing"? A dream that chooses you is forever, while a dream you choose is temporary. Once I'm sold on wanting it, the timetable does not factor in as a "game changer". That doesn't mean you never feel like giving up.

Even if we attempt to repeat someone else's story as if it's our own, it will be without the most important ingredient – you. Your experience is your story, and you'll find a need to draw from it often. It becomes the most personable and endearing side of you. As long as you're being true to your own story, it won't matter in the end, how long it took, or how many people bought in. You will be better for having lived the entire journey. Although I honestly feel some things are long overdue in my life, I still don't believe in shortcuts. We think shortcuts are time savers, when really, they are experience robbers. There are crucial lessons, that if we don't learn them the right way, we must repeat. Not only does it not end up being a short cut of time, but potentially costs us money, frustration, relationships, our integrity, and entire businesses.

Take the option of you not being successful off the table. Your passion should become your life, so much so, that everything you do points to it. Of course, we should all strive to be multi-dimensional, but with a singular vision. If you are eating, sleeping, talking, and walking your vision on a daily basis, it has no choice, but to come to you.

Several months ago I had an encounter with a marketing agent of a book publishing company. Her phone call was to urge me to heavily market the last book I authored. She presented me with packages of different price options to increase my traction in sales. As she talked about the cost and process of getting reviews, and having those reviews advertised in certain magazines, I realized my frustration level was escalating. I understood the information, but it did not sit right with me. Rather than talk about advertising dollars, I asked her to discuss my options for licensing more book titles. She proceeded to tell me that's not how authoring books works. "As an author", she said, "you want your book where it can be seen, talked about, and purchased by the largest number of people". In my head, I totally get that, and I wholeheartedly agree. But that's not how it's been placed in my heart. My reply to her was, "If I'm spending money, I'd rather spend it on the creation of new books. The audience I gain as I continue to write, will appreciate that I have other books, in addition to the one that introduced me to them." We simply agreed to disagree. You must know where you stand, even when your industry has proven strategies that contradict your approach. Just because the way they do it works, doesn't mean it will work for you. It also doesn't mean the way you want to do it won't work.

I'm so grateful for that phone exchange. In that moment, I understood that I had not gone far enough in defining my vision for myself. Unless you can explain it, it's more idea than it is vision.

You won't always be able to find strength in what you've come through, to pull you to victory. For whatever reason, sometimes it's just not enough. Even family support doesn't always prove to be the most effective, depending on your needs. In most communities, you can find listings for disability-specific organizations and groups. It's so vital to create relationships with people that understand, or who may be going through the exact same thing. Family, friends, and colleagues will sympathize, but empathy may be what you need. Disabled people often face a high degree of social isolation. There are talented counselors who can help you sort through some of your frustrations, thoughts, feelings, and even connect you with a support group or therapist. Therapy and support groups are two different things, so do your due diligence to learn the differences between the two.

Support groups can be a wonderful place for caregivers and patients alike, to find unity and comfort in whatever it is you may be going through. More than relationships and connections can be made while attending support group meetings. Challenge yourself to build friendships from these interactions.

Accepting reality means to willfully acknowledge the bitter with the sweet - even when our sweet days are almost nonexistent.

About five years ago, I began noticing some disparities in my sight. I scheduled an appointment with my ophthalmologist, thinking, I simply needed a new prescription for eyeglasses, but it was more complicated. I was referred to a retina specialist, and they discovered improper blood vessels and swelling - obscuring my vision in both eyes. It's called Diabetic Retinopathy. The doctor told me I would need to come into the office every thirty days to receive injections in my eyes to reduce the swelling and slow the growth of the improper blood vessels. I can't adequately express how defeating that moment felt. I was grateful I wasn't being told I would definitely lose all of my ability to see, but this was occurring during an already desolate time in my life. I was literally dying with diabetes. I never denied that it was part of my life, but I hadn't stepped up to make any real changes in my lifestyle. I was more than100 pounds overweight, with no healthy food plan. My obesity fueled sleep apnea, which put extra pressure on my heart, as my breathing would stop and start several times through the night. My blood pressure and cholesterol were high and out of control.

My wife had moved out, and professionally I felt I was in a valley. Optimism has always been one of my assets, but unfortunately, it wasn't propelling me to make the necessary changes. Optimism kept me out of despair, but did not energize me enough to fight the battle.

CHAPTER 3

CORRECTLY ORDER YOUR BATTLES

Everyone has battles. As infants, we enter life with a battle to have our needs met. A baby's cry says, "I want to be fed…, My diaper needs to be changed…, I want to be picked up…, etc."

As we get older and gain more independence, the more battles we face. Unless we address our battles in the right sequence, we risk living life haphazardly. Your methodologies don't have to make sense to everyone, but they must make sense to you. The greatest strategies in the world mean nothing without intrinsic motivation. Once I personally believe something is important, then, and only then will I subscribe to it. There are multiple options for successfully overcoming barriers. Because we are all unique, no one way (order, path) should be mandated for all. Ask any parent who has more than one child. They will tell you how drastically different their children approach identical scenarios. I grew up with five siblings in a 1000 square-foot house. We learned everything together, and were always in one another's space. Yet, amazingly we are polar extremes in some regards. As it relates to school, there's not a lot of room for "individuality" in the traditional classroom. Students are herded in, given required material to read, and told how to think. We grow into adults not realizing we haven't yet given ourselves permission to think, feel, choose, and strategize the way it best works for us. When that blinder gets removed, you will better understand the order in which to number your battles.

WHAT... DOESN'T ALWAYS LEAD TO WHY

Guidance counselors usually encourage adolescents to follow the path of what they enjoy. It's logical that what makes us happy will eventually lead us to discover why it brings us pleasure. I understand the logic, but let's unpack whether or not that is a healthy belief.

Jayla is 14 and she enjoys sewing and creating her own fashions. She doesn't know why, but she really gets a kick out of coming up with outfits she's never seen before. Jayla also has an adventurous palate, and enjoys eating all day long. She is a 372 pound eighth grader. If someone you know goes on a cruise much more often than anyone else you know of, do you say they are addicted to cruising? If a guy fills all of his spare time with basketball, do you call him a basketball addict? Placing a label on Jayla gets her no closer to discovering how to keep her appetite from being so dominant that it controls her health. Labels are what we use to somehow make ourselves feel better; however, they offer no solution. After we're done putting a name on it, we still must get to the WHY. I'm not saying that you will always find "the why". What I am saying is you haven't gone far enough if you haven't sought it out. It's not enough to keep doing things only because you enjoy it. We abort our vision when we fail to ask ourselves, "Is this healthy for me to continue?"

There is a lot of information available with strategies for knowing who you really are.

Although learning your true identity can be a lifelong process, many people discover their true essence early on. I applaud and genuinely admire all those who manage to ground themselves, do the hard work, and embrace the honesty to learn themselves. Even with having that tremendous accomplishment, it's important to understand that 'knowing' and 'confronting' are two separate things. A basketball player can know that he has a very poor jump shot percentage. He can rely on his ability to maneuver inside and only take shots within 3 feet of the basket. He could also work on making key assists that would translate into additional scoring for his team. Or how about the obvious? This athlete could simply confront the issue by investing in the improvement of his shooting. Solving the problem may not be simple, but facing it is the simplest part of the equation. Many people share the opposite opinion, unless or until they learn the skills of confrontation. Confrontation is generally something we avoid, but when it's the boogie man preventing us from sleeping at night, it must be addressed. This may sting, but usually the people we are closely connected to notice it first. If we can get out of pride and start listening to what our friends have to say about us (occasionally) - we could be a lot further down the road.

When I confront that my obscured line of sight has affected my independence, it allows me to be in a better disposition to receive help from others. There are situations that demand we admit that we need help. To some, this may not be a new revelation – but to those of you who are like me, asking for help is almost taboo. Although I am fighting for my wellness, restoration, and continued independence, I desire to live my life at my highest functioning ability. I can become a recluse and avoid uncomfortable scenarios as much as possible, or I can ask for the help I need that will empower me to live my best life. There is a price you pay when you ask for help. People begin to know about your battles. There's also a price you pay when you don't ask for help. You suffer in silence alone - without the opportunity to be a testimony of overcoming a disability. God didn't make us independent. Nor did he make us codependent. He made us interdependent. Our successful reliance is upon all that surrounds us.

Hoarding or Storing?

How you maintain your physical space communicates a lot about where you are headed. An organized filing system is essential for structure and time management. A person's workspace depicts their personality.

When you talk to people who seem to be "all over the place", take a visit to their home or office, and you'll probably see the same. It's not a rule, and I'm partly joking here, but our physical environment plays more of a vital role than we may think. If you have difficulty in being creative or imaginative, check your surroundings. Sometimes the fix is as simple as removing the clutter. Just because you haven't been featured on the show doesn't mean you're not a hoarder. Many of us are hanging on to things we know we'll never use again. If it's causing a distraction, and is not connected to where you are trying to go, get rid of it. How we function in public mirrors the way we live at home. We all have baggage we need to deal with. It's impossible to make it through life without it stacking up. But we've got to set aside time periodically to re-order our lives. I was raised in the Midwest, and we called it spring cleaning, because we had cold winters and hot summers. In the comfort of spring, we practically pulled everything out of the house onto the front lawn or backyard. This allowed us to thoroughly clean the areas inside the house that had been covered by furniture and miscellaneous keepsakes. It was also at this time when my parents decided which items would be allowed back inside and what would be donated or hauled to the street for trash pick-up. I've made the point; decluttering our lives will ultimately support us in maintaining focus for our vision.

CHAPTER 4

TRAUMA AND TRANSFORMATION

Significant losses are known to impact our perspectives. We actually view things through a different lens following a traumatic occurrence. When my father died in 1990, I remember feeling so devastated that life kept on moving. Businesses didn't shut down, and flags weren't lowered to half mass in his honor. To me and my family, he was everything, but his passing meant very little to those who didn't know him personally. His death forced me alive. Instantly every day became sacred. My tolerance for wasting time disappeared. It's not always the loss of a loved one that triggers this feeling. It could be anything we have a strong attachment to. Once our brain makes the connection that that relationship is no longer, it totally shifts how we navigate life. Questions arise to help us order our priorities. And (hopefully) we begin pruning to ensure we are making the most of the time we have.

What loss have you experienced that's causing you to double down, reevaluate, and re-tool? Initially, the pain can feel unbearable. That's the purpose of this book. I hope these words replace anything negative that has tried to root itself in your consciousness, like fear and doubt. It may look different than how you first imagined it, but you can still obtain the vision you have for your life!

My eyesight has regressed significantly since my initial diagnosis. My work commute was 31 miles each way. Just making the round-trip without being involved in an accident, was a miracle in itself. Fortunately, I was able to transfer to a school within 6 miles of my house. That greatly reduced my stress, but after two years, I lost more of my central vision and ability. After 27 years as an educator, I qualified for physical disability leave. Initially, there is a helpless feeling that crashes in like a wave during this type of transition. Getting grounded and confident is a process that starts and stops - depending on the crash of the next wave. I guess that's one reason why it's so important for me to share my truth. When information gets shared as a fictitious scenario, it's hard to emotionally connect to it. But when it's an actual person bearing their soul, it allows others to come out of the dark and say, "me too". We all want to be assured of a life without turmoil. If anyone is making you that promise, don't look for a money-back guarantee; it's not going to happen. But even in the face of the most unimaginable situations - my message is, "live your life!" Go hard!

Wake up to the irony that soon you will have become the stories you tell about your parents. On one hand, it's almost like a cruel joke, but the big 'take away' is to glean everything you can from their successes and failures. Some of our parents made choices that marginally contradicted their upbringing. We make statements in our youthful days like, "I'll never put my children through this." Years later, when we start our own families, our first quest is to parent different than our parents. I include this to express that we are the sum total of all of our experiences. As your charting paths for your family, do so by embracing your whole life. The gap between adolescence and adulthood is so small. In a nanosecond, we go from being a child in the house, to being in charge of the house. A good path forward must take into account where you've been. Some would say, casting vision has nothing to do with the past, and everything to do with the future. Not true. A good visionary relies on information from the past to inform sound decisions going forward. Consistently repeating mistakes with a hopeful demeanor is a devastating cycle, and the definition of insanity.

As I pursue more understanding of myself, I journey closer towards my vision. Along the way, what used to be murky is becoming more defined with clarity. I've always been a writer. I won a writing contest as a child, but in no way did I know then, that I wanted to author books. Words have always fascinated me. It's shocking how you can say the same thing 100 different ways, and illicit a different reaction each time. I am intrigued, not only by how words are put together, but how they are spoken, sung, or interpreted on a page. Songs were my first true gateway to writing. One of my favorite songwriters is Diane Warren. For years, I've been smitten with her ability to wrap resonating lyrics within a pungent melody that totally takes residence in your heart. A well written song is so powerful that it can literally replace an emotion. Songwriting is therapy for me, and I use it as an extension of expressing my thoughts and feelings. I have written more than 3000 songs. As I have continued to evolve, book titles, chapters, and paragraphs are rushing towards me. It's difficult to explain. I didn't wake up one day and decide that I should write books. I simply started lending myself to the process of drafting manuscripts. I am excited to see just how far my evolution will take me.

Regarding your own life's vision - I encourage you to pay close attention to your life. Despite the barriers, don't talk yourself out of what is clearly apparent. I'm paying attention to my life, and I know that words have never lined up for me like this before. I don't view it as a chore or burden, but as a privilege to get words on a page. As I'm authoring books, I must believe in the power of my intention. Believe in the power of yours.

If your life has been spared of trauma, consider yourself truly blessed. Trauma has many different levels, and affects no one exactly the same. If you are a trauma survivor, go even further. Overcome the trauma by not allowing it to creep into dark and hidden places. When we shine a light on what used to oppress us, we take away its power by removing its mystery. If we turn our back on it, the effects from an old wound can resurface in a different form. Remain an advocate to champion the cause, and it will limit traumas of the past from becoming barriers in our future. When I was much heavier, I suffered from gout. I didn't have flareups often, but when it occurred, it took a while to recognize. It was like the pain was trying to be anonymous, presenting as a back spasm, one day, and a tweaked ankle the next. The pain would roam throughout my joints with just enough intensity to cause discomfort - then for no apparent reason, launch an attack on my big toe. In that regard, trauma is a lot like gout. Time goes by, and although you feel far removed from it, it's lurking to invade you. Self-care work must always continue so that we remain healthy psychologically. Thoughts and feelings we refuse to deal with eventually deal with us. Stock your toolbox with what essentially equates to weapons against the debilitating agents of trauma (depression, social anxiety, PTSD, etc.). Even when we label and put a face on trauma, it's difficult to recognize its approach. But when you learn your triggers, trauma doesn't get to go free. Investigating why we're feeling a certain way should be a consistent practice. I hate to be the bearer of bad news, but new trauma has been assigned to each of our lives. We live in a world where seasons change, but fortunately, (no matter what comes) we can choose not to be victims!

CHAPTER 5

GUARD YOUR FOCUS

There is such a thing as allowing your focus to be stolen. This is really huge, because getting our minds to the place of obtaining key focus is usually one of our largest battles. Depending on your entanglements, there's so much vying for our mind's focus minute by minute. As a spouse, employer, employee, or whatever roles you have; people are always competing for our focus. If you are so fortunate to already be on the path of your vision, guard that focus like gold bricks in a vault. It's difficult to help people connected to us understand why we are wired the way we are. We don't half understand it ourselves. Be very cautious about the things and people you add to your life. It's rather easy to unsuspectingly blow up your own life with "time killers". These are appendages that, instead of adding value to our vision, they slow the process. Their involvement is distracting - ciphering the joy from the journey, and diverts the energy from the overall mission. We do this to ourselves sometimes, thinking we are making worthy compromises. One of the hardest lessons to learn is that you become more attractive to others, when you are extremely attracted to your pursuit. In a world inundated with people with no clue about what they want from life - you (the one with a vision) are the unicorn. It's extremely flattering when people acknowledge that they see you, especially if you have felt hidden. But use wisdom and the counsel of good friends when joining your vision to someone else's. The most attractive thing in the world is being comfortable with who you are.

Years ago as a Staff Trainer, I developed a program based on the acronym F.O.C.U.S (Formal Opportunities Causing Unlimited Success). In this training, I emphasized the importance of setting up your thoughts for success. A powerful way to legitimize/stabilize a thought into an actual practice, is to give it an assignment. Once what was part of your imagination is physically being demonstrated in front of you, the brain registers that thought as "successful". Many people will never see the manifestations of their visions due to a lack of focus.

Not only do physical disabilities threaten the pattern of life, but they have the potential to cause one to "lose sight" of who they were before. Don't allow the confident, free-spirited dreamer you once were to become a distant memory. What happened to you does not define who you are. You are stronger than your largest battle, and you must prove that to yourself every day. Unless you believe it, others will find it difficult to connect to your vision. Get in a mirror and gaze until you start remembering your vitality and exuberance. Begin to regain your focus, and get back to the journey you started. I love this quote by Myron Golden, "We give so much energy to the disruption that follows our intention, that we forget the intention that came before the disruption." Don't let it go, or it will haunt you. It surfaces as bitterness and self-loathing. Your body tries to speak from the fear of doubt, but you win that battle by being victorious in your thought life. How we think can easily vacillate, so monitoring what you're digesting takes on an entirely new mandate. Only allow positivity to surround you. You apprehending your vision relies upon your tenacity for being whole. A healthy thought life progresses into how we communicate. What we consistently say about our situation is what ultimately manifests. Stop only saying what your eyes can see, and begin speaking what your heart believes. Faith is now. Let's go!

What doors have your losses opened to you? I'm sure you've heard it said that no two things can occupy the same space. The original context pertains to electrons and atoms, but it is also relevant to our daily existence. Once you are content with what you have, there is no searching for something greater. If something or someone already occupies that space, you have no vacancy. Our brain knows that particular slot is full, and shifts to another focus. Have you ever considered that this new space you're in just might be a new lease on life? How dare I put a positive spin on something negative? I challenge you to do the same. At this moment, let's not focus on what caused us to be here. Let's acknowledge that it really happened, and find ways to be optimistic. If you find that you have vacancies for unoccupied spaces in your life, work on filling them far better than before.

Try to remember what it felt like to be a child with a dream. Money wasn't an obstacle, because you didn't understand the value of it. It was simply something you needed to exchange to get what you wanted. That childlike innocence slips away when we become graduates of the school of hard knocks. Some of us fight longer than others to believe it's still there, but life is good at its job of turning dreamers into realists. There are some who say it hurts more to continue hoping beyond hope. That's not the crowd I'm suggesting you follow. You cannot lower expectations for how things come to you without lowering expectations of yourself. Negative experiences will always try to alter the height of the bar; but the higher we keep it set, the harder we'll fight for what we believe we deserve. There was so much power and energy in that youthful innocence that you must tap into today. Just because you were a child with extremely high hopes doesn't automatically mean you were naïve. The outlook you had for your life in your youth was a seed planted for how you should still imagine your life today. Don't want it because it's popular. Fads change. Want it because you want it. When your motivation for something is pure, your drive for it is unparalleled. It never stops spinning in your mind.

Have you ever spent time around someone completely enthralled with what they do? They are easy to recognize, because they are the ones completely enamored by every part of the job. Not everyone is still chasing their passion. There are people who have captured their dream and living it every day. For some, it's not about fancy cars and a lavish lifestyle. We follow the paths we've been inspired to walk. Every now and then, in all walks of life, I encounter people who go above and beyond the call of duty. I can always tell when they're after more than gratuities, complements, or stellar reviews. Their keen attention to detail shows me when they're in pursuit of my comfort and satisfaction. Passion causes people to go beyond what they do for money.

I recently attended a conference in Atlanta, Georgia, and while booking the flight I scrolled past the option for checking bags, as my plan was to carry on a rolling bag only. A few days before my flight, I received an email from the airline that included a summary of my reservation, and a checklist for being prepared for my flight. Within the summary, it stated that I had not elected to check a bag, and the type of ticket I purchased, doesn't allow for a carry-on bag. In my confusion, I called to speak to a customer service agent. The agent confirmed that I purchased a basic economy ticket which only allows for checked bags at a fee. I asked if she could assist me with adding a checked bag to my reservation, and she said I would have to do that at the counter in the airport when I arrived. After thanking her for the information, I mentioned, "I have a vision impairment. I would appreciate it if there's any way you can facilitate this transaction now over the phone". She responded, "I'm sorry sir. This is something you'll have to do at the counter when you arrive for your flight. Is there anything else I can do to make your customer service experience complete?" After completing the survey, I called again hoping a different agent would be more accommodating. I simply wanted to start over, so I didn't mention that I had already called. After this new agent explained that because of my ticket class, I'll need to pay to check the bag I was planning to carry on, I mentioned my vision impairment and asked if she could do the transaction. After placing me on hold a moment, she said, "Since you're traveling alone, we should make this more convenient for you. You shouldn't have to deal with the baggage claim area once you arrive in Atlanta, so I'm upgrading your ticket to 'preferred'. This ticket allows you to bring your carry-on bag aboard. This ticket also allows you to select your seat. I see an aisle seat near the front of the plane. Would you mind if I reserved that seat for you - for both your outbound and return flights?" Tears began to fall from my eyes.

It was unexpected, and more than I asked for. She had already done enough, then she said, "If you arrive at the airport and feel you need visual assistance, I've listed you for wheelchair assistance. It's better to have it and not need it than to need it and not have it." It was obvious that this young lady put me first that day. She placed herself in my position and offered me the comforts that it would take for her to feel empowered to travel alone in a blurry existence.

CHAPTER 6

BELIEVE AGAIN

Amassing the confidence to brave the world to be yourself, is hard enough to do once. If you are an adult reading this book, most likely you've already celebrated the success of graduating high school, attending college, choosing friends, a career, life partner, etc. None of this is trivial, as these decisions required taking risks. We've analyzed what we've learned about ourselves each step of the way, to make decisions to the best of our ability.

Now things have shifted and it seems your world has been turned upside down.

Although you seemingly have less to work with, your vision is requiring more from you. You are not the same as before, and undoubtingly, your confidence is in question. Can I still perform? Am I still relevant? What will I do if I can't do it this way anymore? I'm sure these only represent a small fraction of the questions you're grappling with. I've got good news for you. You do not have to be who you were before. You are who you are now! Believe in today's you – just like you believed in yourself the first time. Some never start. Celebrate that you've started and endured. Let the goal be to finish!

Some people question whether they should continue a path that has notoriously yielded them nothing. Be sure the dream you're chasing is the dream you actually want. Consider how you got on that road to begin with. Sometimes were overly influenced by good ideas that don't quite meet the requirements of God ideas. Who we are connected to plays a role in what we are connected to. If certain relationships are dissolved, the drive for what you were pursuing together, will definitely be affected. Several questions form. Whose vision was it to begin with? Was that vision originally placed in my heart, or was I later joined to it?

What you're passionate about doesn't have to always make sense. If what you enjoy doing fills a void, you must give it your attention. Don't allow the scope of it to terrify you. If you currently possess all the pieces necessary to erect your dream, it's too small. Dreams should be much larger than we are. Our faith must have something to be energized for. In many ways, apprehending a vision is like a pregnancy. Once you know of it, the responsibility becomes tremendous. It must be safeguarded and nurtured at all times. The vision you have requires research and knowledge, so you have as much information as humanly possible. To successfully birth what you've been carrying, you must place a demand on your physical and mental fitness. Protect your pregnancy by surrounding it with positive energy, and action. Do something every day to ensure the baby is still moving.

If we pledge never to quit, I believe our life solutions inevitably collide into us. The medicine we need must sometimes be administered in doses we can tolerate. I'll never understand why for many of us, it takes getting burned, to learn that fire is truly hot. Something gloomy and tragic shouldn't have to occur, just so we'll snap out of a trance and begin to live correctly. Not being able to read street signs, did it for me. One would think being told you're going blind, would be enough of a shocker. For me, it took more; I had to watch my sight dwindle before deciding to live differently. I hope my transparency helps some of you come out of the closet. You may be surprised to learn you're only hiding from yourself. If your life choices have no Influence on your particular battle, this part isn't for you. Once I began utilizing the tools availed to me, my existence changed. 115 pounds were subtracted from my life. I vow to never carry that weight again, because within it were the excuses that intended to erase me. I still have a sight battle, but my vision is ever so clear. Not only am I not erased, I am boldly becoming the manifestation of who God created me to be. Disability or not, I'll use what I have to go all the way. What can you do differently to increase your territory? What are you watching, reading, saying, and doing - that potentially has you weighed down? God desires us to be good stewards of everything we possess. We have a responsibility to yield the best return to Him for the investment He's made in us.

Belief is such a powerful weapon. It's the seed that germinates the start of every journey. Belief is what snatches us out of bed each morning, destined to reach our goals. It's a position we take, and dare people to chase us off. It's large enough to make us walk down an aisle, and commit our life to another forever. Belief is so big that we can loan some of it to our children until they can start believing for themselves. It's something we have because of what our eyes have witnessed, yet it will grow within us just from our heart's persuasion. It's harder to believe than it is not to, but once you believe, it's difficult to stop. Allow that to work in your favor. Circumstances may have you miles from how you first believed your life would unfold. Plug in again. Your belief is the octane for the engine. It's the protein your muscles need to show definition. Hardship, trauma, and loss wield a giant ax, seeking to chop it down. Our tree of belief has many deep abrasions and has suffered the loss of limbs. Although bruised, rejected, and battered, it stands. It's rejuvenation time! This is the pep rally to stir you to believe again. For some of you reading this book, it's not about you forming a brand-new belief, but you deciding to pick up the belief you had before. It was massive when you first believed it, and it still is today. Go all the way!

If you've never come across anyone dreaming for what you're dreaming for, use that as an authenticator. The uniqueness of your pursuit gives you an additional reason to chase it. Even if you learn that your goals aren't as original as you thought, and there's someone else with the same passion, that has nothing to do with you not going hard. Find excuses to recover ground you may have lost due to embracing the wrong narrative. Every parent's hope is that their children will go beyond their accomplishments and have a greater testimony. Show your children you're not done. Give them lesson 5,082, "How to keep crushing it despite the onset of a disability." This dream was planted in your heart, and if you can't believe for it, you will never see it come to life.

I find that as I am pouring into others, that process pulls me into desiring more from myself. For 27 years, I taught kids the techniques of writing. The ages ranged from 7 to 15, so of course their levels varied greatly. I had to meet them where they were. They enjoyed hearing and reading wonderful stories, but writing their own began with the fundamentals. Some students came to me not knowing how to identify or construct a sentence. They needed to know the importance of punctuation, subject/verb agreement, parts of speech, etc.. Only after embracing the mechanics of writing, can you begin to focus on the creation of your story. It was gratifying to see kids learn the rules for writing, but so rewarding to empower them to tell their story on paper. As an educator, I learned that many students never fully process what they actually believe until they're forced to put it in words on paper. It's because every word must be carefully considered before it's approved to be part of the story. I'm not talking about my approval as the teacher; I mean the student (writer) must confirm for themselves that this is actually what they want to say. When you are required to meditate on your thoughts to the point of writing them down, belief becomes solidified. Revising and editing is a process whereby we mutter sentences over and over until there is a flow that sounds and looks the way we believe.

Habakkuk 2: 2-3

Write down the vision; write it clearly on clay tablets so whoever reads it can run to tell others.

It is not yet time for the message to come true, but that time is coming soon; the message will come true. It may seem like a long time, but be patient and wait for it, because it will surely come; it will not be delayed.

CHAPTER 7

HOW WE SEE OURSELVES

Is it possible that you see yourself in a dimmer light than others do? I'll never forget how shocked I was to find out one of my cousins thought of me as a role model. He's 10 years younger than I am, and I've never really spent a lot of time around him. We grew up in the same circle, and when he was around 21, he mentioned to me that he always looked up to me. He told me about things I had done that he was paying attention to, and that he was watching how I interacted with people.

It really blew me away, as I never considered, I had an audience growing up. Someone is always watching. More importantly, there are people who consider you a hero, that you are totally unaware of. Try to view your life through other people's eyes. They may not all consider you a hero, but I guarantee you, your view of yourself is much lower than the gaze they have. You may not have a giant S on your chest or a cape on your back, but that's no reason not to think highly of yourself. Until you're convinced you deserve the very best life has to offer, you won't demand it or expect to see it come to you. It doesn't just happen. It must be intentional.

Don't allow yourself to be a victim. At some point or another, everyone in life has an opportunity to feel victimized. Even if the merits of your entire timeline portray you as such, "victim" is not a title so easily disposed of. It seeps into your attitude - making you hold people accountable for your lack of progress. It shows up in your work ethic – causing you to intentionally trail behind the pack. Identifying as a victim pulls you off course, into a much slower lane of innovation. This book isn't about race, but some would argue that racial disparity is a disability of its own. The point I'm making is, you very well may be victimized, but never put on the T-shirt. The moment you subscribe to it, is the beginning of surrender. Never give up on the finished painting your imagination has created.

You are considered victorious even before you've won the race. I celebrate you for showing up every day. I honor you for encouraging others with your story of endurance. You're praise-worthy, if only for reading this book; which demonstrates your continued commitment to acquiring knowledge. Celebrate yourself my friend, for you are victorious already. Celebrating what we've overcome energizes us to do more. Imagining yourself as anything other than a winner is equivalent to a stick of butter on a hot stove. Eventually, you will succumb to your environment.

As we become more seasoned, the lens through which we see things changes. Things that mattered the most, somehow matter far less now. When priorities change, almost everything about us becomes different. Priorities greatly affect what we hunger and thirst for. There are some things that we want, but only because we've been programmed to desire them. For instance, someone who has never been on a vacation sees commercials and movies depicting other people's vacation experiences. The person is in awe as they believe these people are experiencing something on a level they can't relate to – as it's totally outside of their experience. I'm sure you're already ahead of me. This person's priority list now includes going on a vacation that matches the advertising they've seen. I find no fault in any of it. I simply want to raise the bar. Obviously my lens as a fifty-five year old is different than my lens of twenty-five. Why can't you and I become the influencers of today? Our priorities shouldn't always be to adopt what the world is selling. We've been there and done that. Stop considering your contribution as done. If you are not actively cultivating a dream, perhaps it's because you are inundated with prioritizing everyone else's.

There is no life where dysfunction has not been on display. If you're ducking and hiding, trying to make sure your secret isn't exposed, you've been found out. Everyone knows you're not perfect, because everyone knows they are not perfect. If this is new information, let's all take a moment to soak it in. I didn't want to use the word disability in this book at all, because that's not a label I subscribe to - but I realized the message would be lost if I didn't include it. We live in a world of assimilation, where people are more comfortable with having a label for the diagnosis, than a prescription for their symptoms.

These pages have included many words about physical and mental battles, but those of course aren't the only obstacles many of us face. We never really know how things will traumatize our life. Routine experiences can cause people to go into shock without them ever knowing. The loss of a pet can evoke confusion, anger, guilt, and denial. Following a woman giving birth are sometimes feelings of intense irritability and depression. Your house being broken into can trigger paranoia and insomnia – even without you having been there when it occurred. Emotional battles can be just as debilitating as physical and mental battles. Although I'm not trying to affix a label to anyone, I am attempting to make the point that the word "disability" has a much broader umbrella than perhaps previously thought.

Are you paying attention to everything you are connected to? Life is always speaking. Knowing when to go forward, backwards, or when to stand still, is always being hinted. We must develop mastery in our observance to put an end to adolescent decision making. If the books and articles I read aren't edging me to unearth the potential within, I must change what I'm reading. If the circle of people I consistently converse with only speak to the hurt, despair, and plight, without discussing hope or a joyful expectation - I must change my circle. Your connections will be the life of you or the death of you. We cannot afford to align ourselves to people and things based on popularity. Don't pledge an allegiance to anything that doesn't pledge to make you whole. How do you know when you're on or off track? Take a moment to list your primary connections on the bottom of a sheet of paper. These should include individuals, groups, and organizations you meet with as often as once per month. At the top of the page, jot down your dream/vision. When you draw lines from your connections, do they align toward your vision? If the lines go anywhere, other than upward, you should carefully reconsider/revisit/redefine that connection.

We don't always get what we deserve. That's a good thing. No doubt we want the proceeds from all the good we are doing, but so very grateful when life gives us a pass on our bad behavior. Take a moment to imagine life differently. What if, from the moment we wake up each day, our every action was recorded? At the end of each week, a highlight reel plays our footage, adding or subtracting grace points based on a composite score. Sure, we'd become more intentional regarding our actions, but that's not how grace works. Why do bad things happen to good people? Is there such a thing as a good or bad person? Why do people with bad lifestyles and bad intentions fare so well? These are all relevant questions that are often debated. No matter your position on these topics, no one is completely invulnerable to the woes of life. It's very frustrating that every action cannot always be traced to a legitimate cause. What knocks on your door tomorrow may be far from what you deserve. We can't always choose what comes into our lives, but how we entertain it is totally on us. Some people, battles, addictions, and illnesses linger and remain when they are energized to do so.

Some of these same culprits vanish when they are forced to vacate.

Just like I don't deserve all of the negative things that try to coexist in my life, I don't deserve all the tremendous blessings I have either. I've done my share of low living, and I thank God for not making me accountable to pay my tab.

CHAPTER 8

BECOME A CHANGE AGENT

Only change influences change. Unless it is demanded, it will not happen. What separates people from machinery is the fact that we are intellectual beings. An unchanging personality is very highly regarded, but we become at risk when we refuse to adapt in a world that is forever changing. The only way to adapt in a changing world, is to remain fluid. Notice I did not say, "adapt TO a changing world". That would suggest us conforming to the world - and that is the posture of so many. Once our eyes are opened to recognize the patterns of change, as a continual inevitability, we can remove ourselves from always having to react to it. Aren't you ready to see the world's system react to the changes you initiate?

Varied experiences contribute to us becoming sterile non-performers. We change just enough to only live the preview of an awesome life.

Sometimes we fear change, even when what we are accustomed to hasn't worked for us. We've become creatures of habit - thinking less while doing more of the same. Many of us lock ourselves into a pattern that feels safe - but only because we are used to it. Is that actually a feeling of safety? Perhaps it's a feeling of being less anxious; because reimagining a whole new way of living can be rather stressful. We must be willing to remain open to different ways of doing things. In the right posture, we can grasp that we don't really see with our eyes. Our eyes are just one of the things our mind uses to see. And if my mind is blind to the possibility, my eyes will be blind to the opportunity.

You'll never find your answers, unless you confront those difficult questions. What was it that stole my confidence? Why am I so afraid to take a risk to go forward? If the aversion to change was part of your character prior to the onset of your disability, it will be increasingly more difficult to overcome this battle now. But I've got great news for you; you are already in the fight for change! Don't let me be your only cheerleader. Set a fire under yourself by reading other authors, who write on the subject of change. Keep uplifting songs with the theme of positive change on your playlist. Subscribe and follow motivational speakers on YouTube. Trace the lines of fear to their source, so you can 'slay the giants' that are still controlling you.

The other day I watched a 1973 episode of Columbo, starring Peter Falk. Columbo was a trenchcoat-wearing LAPD Lieutenant. He was attempting to solve a murder in Los Angeles that actually occurred in San Diego. Two business partners left the office in LA together, taking a drive to a beach house in San Diego for an afternoon of fishing. Keep in mind that only rotary phones with land lines existed during the 70s. Upon arriving, one tells the other to call his wife and tell her he's working late at the office in LA. As he starts to have the operator place the call, his friend abruptly hangs up the phone and says he should call her directly himself, as it will seem more genuine. He makes the call and just after he tells her he's in the office, his friend shoots him so the wife hears it – then he hangs up the phone. As

I'm watching the television, I couldn't help thinking about the many innovative changes that have occurred over the last fifty years. This murderer would not be so elusive in 2023. With current technology, traffic cams would have easily documented both men in the vehicle along their 2 1/2 hour journey from LA to San Diego. Cell phone data would have been in an abundance, as no doubt, the passenger (soon to be victim) would have been googling, browsing, and texting at some point. The wife would've also tracked his phone if she was in doubt about his location. Fifty years ago, telephone operators were actual people. Today we rely on Siri, Alexa, and Google to not only place calls, but for an inexhaustible slew of tasks. It was almost comedic to watch this, because of how far we've come in our ingenuity.

The path towards embracing change begins with owning your issues. There's no requirement to make an announcement, but I'm not ashamed to admit, I have bouts with fear. While I'm trying to consistently make positive changes, how much will my loss of sight change things for me? Although I don't have all the answers, I am thankful for insight that transcends my eyesight.

We stumble over ourselves thinking we are changing when we are actually stuck in the same mindset. Coming out of it really isn't something you can do on your own. Have you ever been on a committee, board, or project with someone who seems to just rub you the wrong way? The process for how they want to do things, and their outlook on strategies frustrates you. Before throwing this person away, you might want to pull them close. Someone very different from you may help you break out of the mold you're stuck in. Electrifying performers like Michael Jackson, Elvis Presley, and Whitney

Houston relied on producers to challenge them in the studio. Yes, even "the greats" need coaches to help them check their attitudes at the door. To create a sound that doesn't completely replicate the last album you recorded, you must render a different kind of performance. It's difficult to change your sound without the right person in your ear. It's not something you're on board with immediately, because you're hearing yourself unlike ever before. That's the part that makes us vulnerable. It's easy to trust who we were and what we've done before, but flipping the script starts that whole trust cycle all over again. I'm not saying all change is good. I'm suggesting the right change, and the correct amount of it.

The pattern most people live is to find a niche, and stay there until being forced off of it. Events such as being fired from a job, having a serious injury, or retiring from the workforce, can force us into a new realm of living. The challenge in living that way is, instead of having one major change to address and pivot for, you're dealing with two. The injury or job change circumstance all by itself is enough for the mind to have to process. If you've never intentionally incorporated change, your brain now has to figure that out as well.

I've been talking about becoming whole. Becoming whole requires changing who we are emotionally, physically, mentally, and financially. Regarding finances, research ways to begin earning money passively. Whether it's intellectual property, royalties (including mineral rights, songs, and books), real estate, investment certificates, etc., there are options available to send your money to work when you can't necessarily go.

A substantial mechanism for change is prayer. Pray that God helps you see things differently; that He opens your eyes to new perspectives, methods, and thoughts.

Lord, show me things I never thought I'd see. Reveal to me what is broken in my life so that I don't waste time trying to repair things that already work. Show me the people who mean me harm, and give me the fortitude to release them from my life. Help me confront my areas of weakness, and allow me the right amount of patience to make the adjustments. Father, teach me forgiveness - for myself, and those I've been carrying in my heart. Only the joy I receive from Your strength affords me the power to take the necessary steps in my life for adequate change. I am asking now for Your joy and peace that passes all understanding. I'm so weary of being ignorant of myself. Help me find the freedom I so desperately need. Unshackle me from the opinions and mannerisms of my peers, and connect me to people and behaviors that foster prosperity. Teach me to have more respect for myself, my time, my talent, and my money. Dear God show me a profound appreciation for the vision You've placed in my heart. Help me find excuses to ensure its manifestation, rather than excuses to fall short. I seal this prayer by denouncing confusion and fear! I ask it all in the name of Jesus; Amen.

CHAPTER 9

CELEBRATE YOUR GREATNESS

This chapter is not from the point of view of you as the underdog. Place those things that are refined and settled about you, center stage. I am so grateful for the aspects of my life that are fixed and secure. We may not achieve greatness in all areas, but possessing greatness is possible. You have it, and it's not vain or arrogant to admit it. Walking in your greatness, enables the confidence needed to become great in other areas.

I opened this book by saying life's playing field is level for all. Excelling in your areas of greatness is what eradicates the wealth gap. It tears down the racial, gender, and age walls. Your greatness takes the spotlight off of what you perceive as a disability, and places the focus on your tremendous ability.

Don't allow your finest attributes to become distorted and reduced to being ineffective. There are amazing things you do naturally that people are studying to emulate you for. I'm not talking about those yet to be discovered facets of your life. I'm speaking of what you are already aware of; those emeralds you downplay as worthless. It's time to talk up your greatness, so your other talents will be stirred within you to come forth.

Don't base your not choosing to celebrate on how small you see the occasion. Take a closer look at what you view as insignificant.

We are usually our hardest critics; always setting the bar just beyond our reach. It's natural to have a desire to accomplish more; but what makes us truly special individuals, are the things we are already great at. This was the nugget my heart caught, that let me know I had to write this book. I can't allow the wave of emotions I feel due to my disability, to have a voice in what I do next. Things only produce after their kind. Fear gives way to fear. Doubt emits doubt. Being anxious radiates and attracts more anxiety. Yes, we are humans with very real emotions, but emotions are what keep many of us bound. Here's another emotion, "anger". We must get angry enough with the emotional cycle, to finally stop allowing our emotions to have a vote. The decision that is best for me, may not be what initially FEELS good to me.

Celebrate that whatever you did wrong is already done. You don't have to repeat it, but you're better for having lived it. Yes, even what's negative about us adds to our greatness. Those who have not put anything to a test, have no way of knowing which direction to take. Being involved and taking risks for what you believe in shortens the distance to the finish line. Get comfortable boasting of your strengths. Every good job interview includes that question. Business owners have trouble placing confidence in people who aren't confident in their own abilities. When filling leadership positions, they know that if you can recognize strengths in yourself, you'll easily identify and encourage the strengths you notice in other employees.

It's not too late to leave a good legacy. As long as you're still alive, there's time to leave a lasting imprint. If you don't feel your life is a testimony of greatness, change it. Begin doing what you admire others for. Partner with a charity or foundation that's creating positive opportunities for others. Often times, joining in leads to ideas and passion to birth things of our own. Excellent collaborations many times are the foundation for prolific advances in our country. Working closely with NAACP, Dr. Martin Luther King, Jr and the Southern Christian Leadership Conference (SCLC) organized sit-ins in public spaces, and the March on Washington for Jobs and Freedom in 1963 which attracted 250,000 people to rally for the civil and economic rights of Black Americans in the nation's capital. Our reach goes so much further when we combine our greatness to the greatness of others.

Mount Rushmore is a project of colossal proportion, ambition, and involved the efforts of nearly 400 men and women. It took 14 years (1927 to 1941) and $989,992,032.00 to blast and carve the likenesses of George Washington, Thomas Jefferson, Theodore Roosevelt, and Abraham Lincoln into the South Dakota Mountain.

Mount Rushmore was intended by its creator, Gutzon Borglum, to be a celebration of not only these four presidents, but also the nation's unprecedented greatness. Borglum remained devoted to the project until his death March 20, 1941, several days before his 74th birthday. The completion of the monument was led by his son, Lincoln - to add the finishing touches on his father's vision. That same year the last face of Theodore Roosevelt was completed. It is estimated that 450,000 tons of rock was removed to unveil what had been in the imagination of this great sculptor. This immense landscape draws nearly 3,000,000 spectators every year.

What is the cost of your greatness? The price you must pay for your vision could very well consume your life. Is that a dealbreaker? You may end up investing more financially than you'll ever receive back from it. Does that cause you to cringe, or hold fast to your dream? Greatness costs!

Since we're all in different stages, for some of you reading this book, this is your reaping season. You've held your course, and your integrity towed the line. The sacrifices you have made for others are irrefutable. You very well could have taken shortcuts, but instead you employed patience and tenacity. You've paid the cost, and now you're in the end zone just waiting for the right pass (book deal, shoe contract, being selected in the draft, lead role in a blockbuster movie). Making it to the end zone and catching the ball for a touchdown are two separate things. Don't just stand there. GET FREE!

Watch how I word this. We must get free to get free. Obviously there's a football analogy in progress. Down after down, you've worked for the necessary yards to get down field. Finally, you're in the red zone, and the defense trails you into the endzone. Thus far none of your receptions have been without massive collision and altercation. Surely your opponent's assignment in the endzone is to deny you the ball at any cost. Your assignment? Get free. Become more dedicated to the task than you've ever been in your life. Create a distinct distance between you and everything else. Create a clear path for your vision to be tossed directly into your arms. THEN you will be free of the **weight** and **wait** of it finally manifesting.

That season is coming for all of us. Just continue being great.

CHAPTER 10

NEVER LOSE YOUR WAY

What is your action plan? Without an outline of processes and procedures, our pursuit is undefined. An action plan provides the nuts and bolts necessary for the fulfillment of the challenge. Expressly communicating what you won't do is just as important as your plan for what you will do. Without those distinctions for your vision, decisions can be made on a whim, that take years to recover from. If you truly believe you're after something God placed in your heart, write it down. It becomes more actionable when it's somewhere other than just your imagination. Even with having action plans, things occur that cause a huge shift in our actionable steps. The purpose of this book has been for that very reason - to discuss the shift. As life throws its subtleties at us, we are confronted with doubling down or letting it go.

A nostalgic mood always helps with being reflective. Usually when we're nostalgic, it brings a sense of calm. The mind seeks to relive moments of inner peace and empowerment. Certain songs instantly transport us back to fits of uncontrollable laughter and jubilation. It's uncanny how music helps time capsule special memories. Periodically it's necessary to conjure up the past to aid us in fortifying our stance. We trek through a mountain of debris along the way to reaching our goals, not always remembering essential elements of why we began. Reestablishing our foundation insurers that we won't lose our way.

Gaining momentum can be very challenging. What do you do when you believe you're right where you should be, but seemingly nothing is happening? We've been groomed to expect lightning-fast results. Staying the course is often the hardest position to maintain. One's outlook can appear mundane while waiting for the next leg of their assignment. This is typically where people let their guard down and become prone to unforced errors. If you are not in doubt as to what your goals are, and you've re-examined why you ever began your journey, you must hold yourself accountable to your action plan. A surefire way of knowing how much strength your vision is gaining is by monitoring the number of people connecting to it. After a certain point, it's no longer just your vision.

Courting or romancing your vision may sound like an odd thing, but I want you to try writing a love letter to your vision. Obviously, the object of your pursuit won't be reading your letter. The schoolteacher in me is giving you an assignment that will hopefully represent more than it does on the surface. Some of you reading this book may still be wrestling with being able to clearly see your vision as a manifestation. If you can't see it in your imagination, how will you know when it manifests? A better question is, "Can it manifest if you can't see it in your imagination?" In your letter, give your vision a personality and human characteristics. For the purpose of this assignment, morph your vision into a person you know well. The more you are able to tie your life and your vision together as partners, the more you will get from this activity. I've written a love letter to my vision as an example.

Dear Vision,

When we first met forty years ago, I was enamored by your beauty. The elegance of your rhyme scheme, and the story you shared drew me in. Your words ignited a melody that began playing in my heart. Your message and my melody danced all night long until the sun came up the next day. Being in your embrace changed me and fueled a fire to write song after song. In the beginning, I wanted our love to pen songs the whole world would sing. But somehow, I became content with our collaboration just remaining between us. On days when it felt like it was me against the world, a studio session with you always brought the calm I needed. It was like therapy. During happy times, we wrote songs of joy. When sadness loomed, we cranked out tearjerkers that provided the peace and healing to move forward. Even when I was wronged, you helped me regain my composure by composing songs of forgiveness. For years, ours has been an impenetrable love. It has been a refuge for me. When there was nothing and no one else, you allowed me to lose myself in you. I once lacked the confidence to say what needed to be said, but you showed me my voice through songwriting. You came to me as a lifeline, but we've grown deep roots together. Vision, you became my Muse and my Ministry.

Just when I thought our love had

reached its peak, you trusted me and revealed yet another layer-another dimension of writing. We've added manuscripts to our repertoire of love. Thank you for whispering book titles and chapters in my ear, that are now flowing like running water. I hope to uplift, inspire, encourage, and entertain readers through my books. Thank you for revealing this powerful medium to me - and for showing me that I have just as much access to the English vernacular as anyone else! Together, we will ultimately empower so many people with the power of our words – the power of our love! I love you Vision, and I'll never do anything to harm you.

Love,

John

A PROPHETIC UTTERANCE

You've sown, nurtured, and protected what once was only part of your imagination. It's no longer in the realm of hope; it's tangible and being birthed. Only now, it affects so many. No one who shall reap from what began in your imagination can afford you losing your way – not now! You must go all the way!

I am concluding this book with this chapter title, "Never Lose Your Way", for a specific reason. It was almost titled, "Never Lose Your Ground". We've all heard, or even used the idiom, 'stay grounded'. When giving advice to someone seemingly moving up the ranks rather quickly, we say to them, stay grounded. When Kelly Rowland told me Destiny's Child would be featured in Will Smith's "Men In Black" video, I told her "stay grounded". Life altering moments can lift you so high into the air, that it's possible to lose the connection for what powers you. This idiom is derived from an electrical engineering principle. Ground or earth is a reference point in an electrical circuit from which voltages are measured (a common return path for an electric current, or a direct physical connection to the earth). Electrical circuits may be connected to ground for several reasons. In Layman's terms, no ground connection means no current flows in a building's electrical circuit. A very weak connection between a building's electrical system and earth can result in power loss when there is a load placed on the system.

Staying grounded will assist you in not losing your way. When you're tapped to play the starring role in a beastiality film, paying you $100 million, being grounded, will help you in being responsive to your morals. Without well-intentioned connections, it's possible to justify decisions until there's no you left. I hope this book is broadening your capacity to believe. Many of you reading this book have never made vision-killing morality choices simply because you've not had the opportunity. Be careful not to judge those who live in the scrutiny of the spotlight. It's easy to condemn someone's choices when no one is paying attention to yours. Take this time to reestablish how and what you believe so you can reaffirm your commitments and stay grounded. Expect the enormity of your vision to thrust you center stage. Get ready for it! It's coming! Respond in a way that extends the life of your vision!

ABOUT THE AUTHOR

DR. JOHN DAVID MCCONNELL

Dr. John David McConnell is the owner of Prolyric Productions Publishing Company. Born and raised in Kansas City Kansas, John received his Bachelor of Science degree at Saint Mary College in Leavenworth, Kansas. John taught grades 2 through 8 over the span of his 27-year career as a public-school educator. 20 of those years were with the Houston Independent School District.

In 2016 John received his doctorate in sacred music from Christian Bible Institute & Seminary. His war chest of badges includes Christian, father of two sons, educator, actor, singer, songwriter, worship-leader, Certified Christian Counselor, and author. John exited his teaching career in 2022, and is currently pursuing his literary and songwriting careers full-time.

To Contact John McConnell: Johndmac4@ aol.com 832-865-0260 Photography by: Stanton Trueheart

Printed in the United States
by Baker & Taylor Publisher Services